The 5-Minute Gratitude Journal

The 5-Minute Gratitude Journal

GIVE THANKS,
PRACTICE POSITIVITY,
FIND JOY

SOPHIA GODKIN, PhD

ROCKRIDGE
PRESS

For general information on our other products and services or to obtain technical support, please contact our Customer Care Department within the United States at (866) 744-2665, or outside the United States at (510) 253-0500.

Rockridge Press publishes its books in a variety of electronic and print formats. Some content that appears in print may not be available in electronic books, and vice versa.

Interior and Cover Designer: Lisa Forde
Art Producer: Hannah Dickerson
Editor: Sean Newcott
Production Editor: Ruth Sakata Corley
Author photo courtesy of CWRaw Designs

ISBN: Print 978-1-64739-719-7
eBook 978-1-64739-720-3

R0

**FOR MY FRIEND
PRIEL SCHMALBACH,**
*who was the embodiment of
a full and grateful heart.*

Introduction

Welcome to *The 5-Minute Gratitude Journal*—your peace-of-mind-inducing companion for the next few weeks, months, or perhaps, years of your life. My name is Dr. Sophia Godkin and I'm what you could call a "gratitude believer." As a health psychologist, happiness coach, and positive psychology professor, I'm often asked, "What *is* the secret to happiness?" My reply? The secret to happiness is simple. And it begins with gratitude.

Gratitude is the feeling of appreciation we have for the people, experiences, and things in our lives that have helped or supported us in some way. You know you've encountered gratitude when you feel alive, joyful, and satisfied with your life just as it is in the moment. You know you've been cultivating gratitude for some time when you feel personally more resilient, content, and optimistic, and also feel all-around more compassionate, kind, and connected to others.

My personal journey with gratitude began early on in adulthood when several life challenges revealed the inextricable link between my mindset and my happiness—the more dissatisfied or unappreciative I was, the more difficult it was to access positive emotions. My discovery of this connection led me to seek out the simple but effective strategies that scientists and spiritual teachers alike report to have the greatest happiness-boosting benefits. Through research and personal practice, I quickly learned that gratitude is a powerful tool unlike any other. When practiced occasionally, gratitude has a noticeable impact on our day-to-day lives; when practiced consistently, it can transform our lives for the better in remarkable ways that we couldn't have imagined.

It is said that all good habits start small. If so, journaling about gratitude is the perfect way to turn gratitude from an occasional occurrence into a consistent practice. The more you do it, the more it becomes a habit. The more it becomes a habit, the easier it becomes for you to do it every day. The best part? Even the busiest people are never too busy to benefit from journaling for just five minutes a day.

The Power of Gratitude

Gratitude is a practice that delivers universal benefits. According to Robert Emmons, the world's leading expert on gratitude, there is not one area of life that doesn't improve when we use gratitude as the lens from which to view it.

When it comes to emotional well-being, people who practice gratitude consistently tend to be happier, more optimistic, and more satisfied with life than those without a consistent practice. When it comes to social relationships and interactions, those with a consistent gratitude practice typically feel less lonely and isolated, are able to strengthen intimate relationships, and embrace feeling more outgoing, forgiving, compassionate, and generous. People who practice gratitude, even for just five minutes a day, also tend to experience improved physical health—lower blood pressure, stronger immune systems, longer and deeper sleep, and fewer aches and pains. Additionally, gratitude and positive emotions operate in a synergistic manner: gratitude strengthens our ability to cope with stress and encourages us to live in and celebrate the present, while positive emotions like happiness help us recognize who or what to be grateful for each day.

How to Use This Journal

The 5-Minute Gratitude Journal makes it easy and enjoyable to develop a daily gratitude practice. Whenever you have five minutes, simply open your journal, fill in the date, and begin writing. Before you know it, you'll feel lighter, happier, and more optimistic. Here are a few tips on how to navigate the features of this gratitude journal and how you can get the most out of your journal-writing experience.

THOUGHT-PROVOKING PROMPTS. Each dated entry contains four thought-provoking prompts meant to inspire you to notice things, big and small, that you may otherwise take for granted each day. As you write, *stay in the feeling of gratitude* by taking a moment to savor the person, experience, or thing for which you are grateful.

INSPIRATIONAL QUOTES. As you make your way through the journal, you'll encounter inspirational quotes from wise people, from all walks of life, who understand the power of gratitude and are living it daily. By reading their unique perspectives on gratitude, you are invited to understand and appreciate why gratitude is such an essential part of living a happy, healthy, and meaningful life.

POWERFUL AND POSITIVE AFFIRMATIONS. Another helpful tool on your journey are affirmations—statements meant to help you cultivate an optimistic and positive outlook on yourself and on your life. Simply repeat an affirmation to yourself whenever you need a "mindset reset" to help you get inspired, feel motivated, or bring about positive thoughts and actions throughout your day.

Each journal entry—thoughtfully designed to transport you into a state of gratitude—takes just five minutes to complete. Thankfully, five minutes is all it takes to begin and maintain a regular practice of gratitude that will benefit you in many ways. Before you know it, grateful won't just be something that you *want to be*; it will be something that you *are*!

Congratulations on taking the first step to becoming a more grateful you. Whatever your personal goals, whatever your individual desires, and whatever your reasons for wanting to foster an attitude of gratitude, this journal is here to help you on your way. You know what life can be like *without* a consistent practice of gratitude, so what do you say we see what life can be like *with* one?

Now and then it's good to pause in our pursuit
of happiness and just be happy.

– GUILLAUME APOLLINAIRE

One reason my life is already great ___nintendo switch___

_____

_____

Someone whose presence makes my life sweeter ___Emma___

_____

_____

Something I get to do today that I've always wanted to do _____
___go to sleep early___

_____

One beautiful reason to be happy right now _____
___the weather is nice___

_____

I AM JUST BEGINNING
THE BEST PART OF MY LIFE.

Once we begin to look for what's right, our lives begin spinning in unimaginably exciting new directions.

– PAM GROUT

An unforgettable memory I treasure Barrood in Paris

One of the best parts about being me I can enjoy myself alone

Something I currently have that I've always wanted Fire Emblem: Three Houses

A new door that opened for me recently Emma's coming to the beach with me

I KNOW THAT WHATEVER IS MEANT
FOR ME IS MAKING ITS WAY TO ME.

DATE

_____ / _____ / _____

The place to be happy is here. The time to be happy is now.

– ROBERT G. INGERSOLL

A person, place, or thing that makes my life easier and happier ____

_____

_____

Someone who makes my life better just by being in it _____

_____

_____

Something that worked out much better than I'd hoped _____

_____

_____

Something in my life that makes it worth living _____

_____

_____

MY LIFE IS FULL OF WONDERFUL THINGS
AND I AM LOVING EVERY MINUTE OF IT.

DATE

_____ / _____ / _____

Wear gratitude like a cloak and it will feed every corner of your life.

– RUMI

A quality of one of my closest friends that I absolutely love _____

_____

_____

What I appreciate most about this moment _____

_____

_____

An opportunity I have today that I only dreamt about having

previously _____

_____

Something about me that's worth celebrating _____

_____

_____

MY CAPACITY FOR JOY IS LIMITLESS.
MY POTENTIAL FOR LOVE IS INFINITE.

DATE

_____ / _____ / _____

Practicing gratitude is how we acknowledge that there's enough and that we're enough.

– BRENÉ BROWN

Someone who helped me get to where I am today _____

_____

_____

A sight, sound, or feeling that reminds me why life is so amazing

_____

_____

One way my life is better now than I ever expected it to be _____

_____

_____

A challenging experience that helped me grow into a better

version of myself_____

_____

I AM ABOUT TO BE HAPPIER
THAN I HAVE EVER BEEN.

DATE

_____ / _____ / _____

The root of joy is gratefulness . . . It is not joy that makes
us grateful; it is gratitude that makes us joyful.

– BROTHER DAVID STEINDL-RAST

Someone I get to spend time with today _____

_____

_____

A reason to smile right now _____

_____

_____

A valuable lesson I learned from a difficult situation _____

_____

_____

Something that went right today _____

_____

_____

I HAVE EVERYTHING I NEED TO
LIVE A FULL AND SATISFYING LIFE.

*Trade your expectation for appreciation and
the world changes instantly.*

– TONY ROBBINS

So far, what I love most about today _____

_____

_____

Something I have that makes it easy to love my life _____

_____

_____

Someone who's given me hope on a bad day _____

_____

_____

Something I wake up to that reminds me what a gift it is to be alive

_____

_____

I AM THANKFUL FOR WHERE I'VE BEEN,
HAPPY WITH WHERE I AM, AND EXCITED
ABOUT WHERE I AM GOING.

DATE

_____ / _____ / _____

If you start looking for the good things in your life, you just might be surprised at how many of them you really have.

– STACIE MARTIN

Something great about today that makes me look forward to

tomorrow _____

_____

One way I'm already living the life I want _____

_____

_____

A second chance I've been given _____

_____

_____

Someone or something that makes me smile like a kid again _____

_____

_____

I AM LEARNING
AND GROWING INTO A POSITIVE,
FULFILLING FUTURE.

Starting today, I need to forget what's gone, appreciate what still remains, and look forward to what's coming next.

– UNKNOWN

Something I believe in that gives me hope day to day _____

_____

_____

The best moment of today _____

_____

_____

A privilege I have that, until now, I've taken for granted _____

_____

_____

A breakdown that led me to a breakthrough _____

_____

_____

LIFE IS A JOURNEY AND I AM GROWING
WISER, STRONGER, AND BRAVER BY THE DAY.

DATE

_____ / _____ / _____

*I hope there are days when you fall
in love with being alive.*

– UNKNOWN

Something I can experience or imagine that inspires me _____

_____

_____

An experience I cherish because it taught me something valuable

_____

_____

Something uplifting that someone said or did _____

_____

_____

One clear reason to appreciate the person I've become _____

_____

_____

I AM SINCERELY GRATEFUL FOR WHO
I AM, WHERE I AM, AND WHAT I HAVE.

DATE

_____ / _____ / _____

When you love what you have, you have everything you need.

– UNKNOWN

One simple reason to be grateful for living where I live _____

_____

_____

A time when I felt I was in the right place at the right time _____

_____

_____

Something great about today that I may have overlooked

yesterday _____

_____

A little thing someone did that meant a lot to me _____

_____

_____

 EVERY DAY, I AM GRATEFUL TO GROW,
NO MATTER HOW SLOWLY.

DATE

_____ / _____ / _____

I have found that if you love life, life will love you back.

– ARTHUR RUBINSTEIN

Someone or something that made today a good day _____

_____

_____

Someone I don't want to miss an opportunity to say thank you to

_____

_____

A recent event that confirms things are working out for me _____

_____

_____

Something that gives my life meaning _____

_____

_____

I TRUST THAT EVERYTHING HAPPENING
NOW IS HAPPENING FOR MY BENEFIT.

DATE

_____ / _____ / _____

The more you express gratitude for what you have, the more likely you will have even more to express gratitude for.

– ZIG ZIGLAR

Something that gives my life pleasure _____

_____

_____

An ability that I am fortunate to have _____

_____

_____

A choice I can make that not everyone gets to make _____

_____

_____

The greatest benefit of being alive right now _____

_____

_____

WHERE I'VE BEEN HAS BEEN GREAT.
WHERE I'M GOING WILL BE EVEN BETTER.

DATE

_____ / _____ / _____

*The single greatest thing you can do to change your life today
would be to start being grateful for what you have right now.
And the more grateful you are, the more you get.*

– OPRAH WINFREY

The moment I felt most alive and fully myself this week _____

_____

_____

A need I have that is being met today _____

_____

_____

An unforgettable memory I treasure _____

_____

_____

One of the best parts about being me _____

_____

_____

EACH DAY, I AM DISCOVERING NEW,
SIMPLE WAYS TO CREATE A LIFE THAT I LOVE.

DATE

_____ / _____ / _____

A beautiful day begins with a beautiful mindset . . .
Start thinking about what could go right. Better yet,
think of everything that already is right.

– JOHN GEIGER

One reason my life is already great _____

_____

_____

A new door that opened for me recently _____

_____

_____

Something in my life that makes it worth living _____

_____

_____

Someone I get to spend time with today _____

_____

_____

I HAVE A WELL-BALANCED
POINT OF VIEW; I CAN FIND THE GOOD
IN EVERY SITUATION.

DATE

_____ / _____ / _____

I opened two gifts this morning.
They were my eyes.

– ZIG ZIGLAR

A person, place, or thing that makes my life easier and happier ____

_____

_____

Someone who helped me get to where I am today _____

_____

_____

A quality of one of my closest friends that I absolutely love _____

_____

_____

Something that went right today _____

_____

_____

I OPEN MY MIND AND HEART
TO NEW OPPORTUNITIES AND
UNEXPECTED POSSIBILITIES.

DATE

_____ / _____ / _____

When anything good happens to you in your day, give thanks.
It doesn't matter how small it is, say thank you.

– RHONDA BYRNE

Someone whose presence makes my life sweeter _____

_____

_____

What I appreciate most about this moment _____

_____

_____

A sight, sound, or feeling that reminds me why life is so amazing

_____

_____

A privilege I have that, until now, I've taken for granted _____

_____

_____

THE PAST IS OVER AND GONE.
I CREATE MY FUTURE WITH WHAT I CHOOSE
TO FOCUS ON AND THINK ABOUT TODAY.

DATE

_____ / _____ / _____

*Things turn out best for people who make
the best of the way things turn out.*

– JOHN WOODEN

Something I get to do today that I've always wanted to do _____

_____

_____

One way my life is better now than I ever expected it to be _____

_____

_____

A reason to smile right now _____

_____

_____

Something great about today that makes me look forward to

tomorrow _____

_____

EVERY DECISION
I MAKE LEADS ME SOMEWHERE
WONDERFUL.

DATE

_____ / _____ / _____

The sun is perfect and you woke this morning . . .
You have a name, and someone wants to call it. Five fingers on
your hand and someone wants to hold it . . . If we start there,
everything, for a moment, is right in the world.

– WARSAN SHIRE

One beautiful reason to be happy right now _____

_____

_____

Something I currently have that I've always wanted _____

_____

_____

Someone who makes my life better just by being in it _____

_____

_____

Something about me that's worth celebrating _____

_____

_____

IT IS A JOY TO RELATE TO
MYSELF AND THE WORLD AROUND ME
IN KIND AND LOVING WAYS.

DATE

_____ / _____ / _____

No amount of regret can change the past,
no amount of worrying can change the future, but any
amount of gratitude can change the present.

– UNKNOWN

Something that worked out much better than I'd hoped _____

_____

_____

An opportunity I have today that I only dreamt about having

previously _____

_____

A challenging experience that helped me grow into a better version

of myself _____

_____

Something that went right today _____

_____

_____

I ENGAGE WITH LIFE WITH A
DEEP BREATH, AN OPEN MIND, AND
A GRATEFUL HEART.

DATE

_____ / _____ / _____

Every day, think as you wake up, today I am fortunate to be alive,
I have a precious human life, I am not going to waste it.

– DALAI LAMA

A valuable lesson I learned from a difficult situation _____

_____

_____

So far, what I love most about today _____

_____

_____

A second chance I've been given _____

_____

_____

Something I have that makes it easy to love my life _____

_____

_____

I APPROACH EACH MOMENT OF MY DAY
WITH WONDER, CURIOSITY,
AND GRATITUDE.

DATE

_____ / _____ / _____

Every now and then it's good to stop climbing and
appreciate the view from right where you are.

– LORI DESCHENE

Something I wake up to that reminds me what a gift it is to be alive

_____

_____

The best moment of today _____

_____

_____

A breakdown that led me to a breakthrough _____

_____

_____

One clear reason to appreciate the person I've become _____

_____

_____

EVERYTHING THAT HAPPENS,
FAILURE OR SUCCESS,
HELPS ME BECOME A BETTER ME.

DATE

_____ / _____ / _____

*Expressing gratitude for the miracles in your world is one of the best
ways to make each moment of your life a special one.*

– WAYNE DYER

One way I am already living the life I want _____

_____

_____

Someone or something that makes me smile like a kid again _____

_____

_____

An experience I cherish because it taught me something valuable

_____

_____

A recent event that confirms that things are working out for me

_____

_____

I EMBRACE UNCERTAINTY
AND LET LIFE SURPRISE ME IN MANY
WONDERFUL WAYS.

DATE

_____ / _____ / _____

Gratitude creates space for something new. It creates room for healing to occur, intentions to show up, miracles to happen.

– PAM GROUT

Someone who's given me hope on a bad day _____

_____

_____

One simple reason to be grateful for living where I live _____

_____

_____

A little thing someone did that meant a lot to me _____

_____

_____

An ability that I am fortunate to have _____

_____

_____

EVERYTHING I IMBUE WITH GRATITUDE
TODAY HELPS ME CREATE A MORE
BLISSFUL TOMORROW.

DATE

_____ / _____ / _____

Every morning when I open my curtains for that first look at the day . . . my heart swells with gratitude. I get another chance.

– OPRAH WINFREY

Something I believe in that gives me hope day to day _____

_____

_____

A time when I felt I was in the right place at the right time _____

_____

_____

Something that gives my life meaning _____

_____

_____

The greatest benefit of being alive right now _____

_____

_____

I LOOK BACKWARD
WITH A SMILE, AND I LOOK
FORWARD WITH HOPE.

DATE

_____ / _____ / _____

The struggle ends when gratitude begins.

– NEALE DONALD WALSCH

Something I can experience or imagine that inspires me _____

_____

_____

A choice I can make that not everyone gets to make _____

_____

_____

Someone I don't want to miss an opportunity to say thank you to

_____

_____

Something or someone that made today a good day _____

_____

_____

LIFE IS A SERIES OF TINY MIRACLES.
TODAY, I CHOOSE TO NOTICE AND BE
THANKFUL FOR THEM ALL.

There is so much to be grateful for; just open your eyes.

– UNKNOWN

Something uplifting that someone said or did _____

_____

_____

One reason my life is already great _____

_____

_____

Something I get to do today that I've always wanted to do _____

_____

_____

A new door that opened for me recently _____

_____

_____

WITH A GRATEFUL HEART,
I EASILY CREATE A LIFE I LOVE.

DATE

_____ / _____ / _____

Forget yesterday—it has already forgotten you.
Don't sweat tomorrow—you haven't even met. Instead, open your
eyes and your heart to a truly precious gift—today.

Something great about today that I may have overlooked

yesterday _____

_____

Something that gives my life pleasure _____

_____

_____

Someone whose presence makes my life sweeter _____

_____

_____

An unforgettable memory I treasure _____

_____

_____

I HAVE ENOUGH
AND AM ENOUGH.

DATE

_____ / _____ / _____

The secret to having it all is knowing you already do.

– UNKNOWN

One beautiful reason to be happy right now _____

_____

_____

Something I currently have that I've always wanted _____

_____

_____

A person, place, or thing that makes my life easier and happier ___

_____

_____

Something about me that's worth celebrating _____

_____

_____

THE NEXT INSPIRATION, SOLUTION,
OR INSIGHT I NEED
IS ALWAYS RIGHT WHERE I AM.

DATE

_____ / _____ / _____

Appreciate everything . . . Appreciate your balance.
Appreciate your life. Appreciate yourself.

– UNKNOWN

One of the best parts about being me _____

_____

_____

Someone who makes my life better just by being in it _____

_____

_____

A quality of one of my closest friends that I absolutely love _____

_____

_____

An opportunity I have today that I only dreamt about having

previously _____

_____

LOVE IS
EVERYWHERE I AM.

DATE

_____ / _____ / _____

A moment of gratitude makes a difference in your attitude.

– BRUCE WILKINSON

Something that worked out much better than I'd hoped _____

_____

_____

What I appreciate most about this moment _____

_____

_____

Something in my life that makes it worth living _____

_____

_____

Someone who helped me get to where I am today _____

_____

_____

YES, I CAN.

DATE

_____ / _____ / _____

Gratitude is one of the sweet shortcuts to finding peace of mind and happiness inside. No matter what is going on outside of us, there's always something we could be grateful for.

– BARRY NEIL KAUFMAN

A sight, sound, or feeling that reminds me why life is so amazing

_____

_____

One way my life is better now than I ever expected it to be _____

_____

_____

A challenging experience that helped me grow into a better

version of myself _____

_____

Someone I get to spend time with today _____

_____

_____

I CHOOSE TO BE GRATEFUL BECAUSE I LOVE
HOW BEING GRATEFUL MAKES ME FEEL.

*There are always flowers for
those who want to see them.*

– HENRI MATISSE

A reason to smile right now _____

_____

_____

A valuable lesson I learned from a difficult situation _____

_____

_____

Something that went right today _____

_____

_____

Something I have that makes it easy to love my life _____

_____

_____

I HAVE BEEN BLESSED WITH UNIQUE
TALENTS AND ABILITIES, AND I SEE, VALUE,
AND USE THEM TODAY.

DATE

_____ / _____ / _____

In life, one has a choice to take one of two paths: to wait for some special day—or to celebrate each special day.

– RASHEED OGUNLARU

So far, what I love most about today _____

_____

_____

Something I wake up to that reminds me what a gift it is to be alive

_____

_____

One way I am already living the life I want _____

_____

_____

Someone who's given me hope on a bad day _____

_____

_____

I AM LEARNING TO BE IN LOVE
WITH MY LIFE. EVERY MINUTE OF IT.

DATE

_____ / _____ / _____

Be content with what you have; rejoice in the way things are. When you realize there is nothing lacking, the whole world belongs to you.

– LAO TZU

Something great about today that makes me look forward to

tomorrow _____

_____

Something I believe in that gives me hope day to day _____

_____

_____

A privilege I have that, until now, I've taken for granted _____

_____

_____

A breakdown that led me to a breakthrough _____

_____

_____

I AM AT PEACE WITH MY PAST,
DEEPLY SATISFIED WITH MY PRESENT,
AND EXCITED ABOUT MY FUTURE.

DATE

_____ / _____ / _____

Enough is a feast.

– BUDDHIST PROVERB

The best moment of today _____

_____

_____

Someone or something that makes me smile like a kid again _____

_____

_____

A second chance I've been given _____

_____

_____

Something I can experience or imagine that inspires me _____

_____

_____

I AM A PRODUCT OF MY CHOICES,
NOT OF MY CIRCUMSTANCES—AND GOOD
CHOICES ARE EASY FOR ME TO MAKE.

DATE

_____ / _____ / _____

Celebrate what you want to see more of.

– TOM PETERS

An experience I cherish because it taught me something valuable

_____

_____

One clear reason to appreciate the person I've become _____

_____

_____

A time when I felt I was in the right place at the right time _____

_____

_____

One simple reason to be grateful for living where I live _____

_____

_____

I LOVE WHAT I SEE IN ME.

DATE

_____ / _____ / _____

When it comes to life, the critical thing is whether you take
things for granted or take them with gratitude.

– G. K. CHESTERTON

Something or someone that made today a good day _____

_____

_____

A recent event that confirms things are working out for me _____

_____

_____

A little thing someone did that meant a lot to me _____

_____

_____

Someone I don't want to miss an opportunity to say thank you to

_____

_____

THERE IS ABSOLUTELY NOTHING
WRONG, AND THERE IS EVERYTHING
RIGHT, WITH THIS MOMENT.

DATE

_____ / _____ / _____

The world has enough beautiful mountains and meadows,
spectacular skies and serene lakes . . . What the world needs more
of is people to appreciate and enjoy it.

– MICHAEL JOSEPHSON

Something that gives my life meaning _____

_____

_____

An ability that I am fortunate to have _____

_____

_____

A choice I can make that not everyone gets to make _____

_____

_____

The greatest benefit of being alive right now _____

_____

_____

I LIVE IN A NATURAL STATE OF
WELL-BEING AND INNER PEACE.

DATE

_____ / _____ / _____

We can only be said to be alive
in those moments when our hearts are conscious
of our treasures.

– THORNTON WILDER

The moment I felt most alive and fully myself this week _____

_____

_____

A need I have that is being met today _____

_____

_____

One reason my life is already great _____

_____

_____

Someone whose presence makes my life sweeter _____

_____

_____

EVERY DAY I WAKE UP AND AM
THANKFUL SIMPLY FOR BEING ALIVE.

DATE

_____ / _____ / _____

When life is sweet, say thank you and celebrate. And when life is bitter, say thank you and grow.

– SHAUNA NIEQUIST

A skill I have that benefits me in an important way _____

_____

_____

One simple pleasure I value _____

_____

_____

The best part of today _____

_____

_____

An unforgettable memory I treasure _____

_____

_____

DOORS OF OPPORTUNITY ARE ALL AROUND
ME TODAY, JUST WAITING TO BE OPENED.

DATE

_____ / _____ / _____

Love absolutely everything that ever happens in your life.

– PAUL CANTALUPO

One reason I cherish this time of year _____

_____

_____

A freedom I have that I once took for granted _____

_____

_____

What I love most about my community _____

_____

_____

A little thing someone did that meant a lot to me _____

_____

_____

MY PROBLEMS AND CHALLENGES ARE
NOTHING BUT A BLESSING IN DISGUISE.

DATE

_____ / _____ / _____

Joy is a decision, a really brave one,
about how you're going to respond to life.

– WESS STAFFORD

A valuable lesson I learned from a difficult conversation _____

_____

_____

A new door that opened for me recently _____

_____

_____

Something that gives my life meaning _____

_____

_____

Something about myself I would never change _____

_____

_____

I AM SURROUNDED BY MANY GOOD THINGS,
BIG AND SMALL, EVERY DAY OF MY LIFE.

DATE

_____ / _____ / _____

Appreciation can make a day,
even change a life.

– MARGARET COUSINS

What I appreciate most about this moment _____

_____

_____

An opportunity I have today that I only dreamt about having

previously _____

_____

Something about me that's worth celebrating _____

_____

_____

Someone who helped me get to where I am today _____

_____

_____

LIFE NATURALLY AND FREELY BRINGS TO ME
ALL THAT I NEED WHEN I NEED IT.

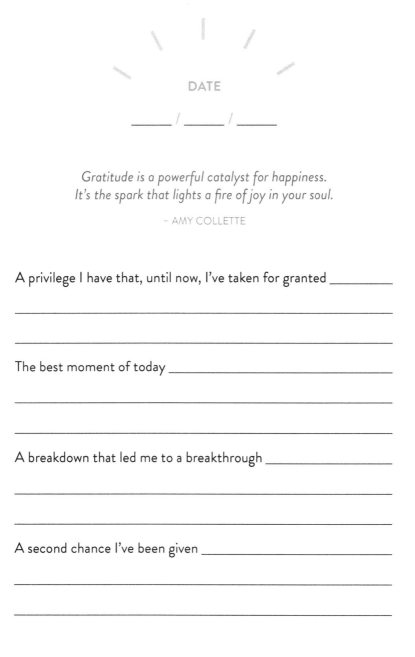

DATE

_____ / _____ / _____

Gratitude is a powerful catalyst for happiness.
It's the spark that lights a fire of joy in your soul.

– AMY COLLETTE

A privilege I have that, until now, I've taken for granted _____

_____

_____

The best moment of today _____

_____

_____

A breakdown that led me to a breakthrough _____

_____

_____

A second chance I've been given _____

_____

_____

I AM CONSTANTLY EVOLVING INTO A
BETTER PERSON, FRIEND, AND MEMBER
OF MY COMMUNITY.

DATE

_____ / _____ / _____

*Life does not have to
be perfect to be wonderful.*

– ANNETTE FUNICELLO

A little thing someone did that meant a lot to me _____

_____

_____

Someone I don't want to miss an opportunity to say thank you to

_____

_____

A recent event that confirms that things are working out for me

_____

_____

Something that gives my life meaning _____

_____

_____

TODAY I FOCUS ON WHAT I CAN CONTROL
AND LET GO OF ALL THE REST.

*Stop worrying about the potholes
in the road and enjoy the journey.*

– BABS HOFFMAN

Something I get to do today that I've always wanted to do _____

_____

_____

One beautiful reason to be happy right now _____

_____

_____

An unforgettable memory I treasure _____

_____

_____

One of the best parts about being me _____

_____

_____

I HAVE EVERYTHING
I NEED TO MAKE THIS DAY
A GOOD ONE.

DATE

_____ / _____ / _____

The best part about life? Every morning you have a new opportunity to become a happier version of yourself.

– KELLI PEASE

Something I currently have that I've always wanted _____

_____

_____

A new door that opened for me recently _____

_____

_____

A person, place, or thing that makes my life easier and happier ____

_____

_____

Someone who makes my life better just by being in it _____

_____

_____

I AM BALANCED IN MY ABILITY TO
BOTH APPRECIATE WHAT I HAVE AND
WORK ON WHAT I WANT.

DATE

_____ / _____ / _____

If you look the right way, you can see that the whole world is a garden.

– FRANCES HODGSON BURNETT

A sight, sound, or feeling that reminds me why life is so amazing

_____

_____

One way my life is better now than I ever expected it to be _____

_____

_____

A challenging experience that helped me grow into a better

version of myself _____

_____

Someone I get to spend time with today _____

_____

_____

IT'S EASY TO FIND MOMENTS OF PLEASURE
AND MEANING WITHIN MY DAY.

DATE

_____ / _____ / _____

Never let things you want make you forget the things you have.

– SANCHITA PANDEY

A reason to smile right now _____

_____

_____

A valuable lesson I learned from a difficult situation _____

_____

_____

So far, what I love most about today _____

_____

_____

Something I have that makes it easy to love my life _____

_____

_____

EVERYTHING IN MY LIFE UNFOLDS IN
ITS RIGHT AND PERFECT WAY.

DATE

_____ / _____ / _____

I am not afraid of tomorrow,
for I have seen yesterday and I love today.

– WILLIAM ALLEN WHITE

Something I wake up to that reminds me what a gift it is to be alive

_____

_____

One way I am already living the life I want _____

_____

_____

Someone who's given me hope on a bad day _____

_____

_____

What went right today _____

_____

_____

WHY FOCUS ON
WHAT I LACK WHEN I CAN FOCUS ON
ALL THAT I HAVE?

DATE

_____ / _____ / _____

Gratitude is the sweetest thing in a seeker's life—
in all human life. If there is gratitude in your heart, then there
will be tremendous sweetness in your eyes.

– SRI CHINMOY

Something uplifting that someone said or did _____

_____

_____

One clear reason to appreciate the person I've become _____

_____

_____

An experience I cherish because it taught me something valuable

_____

_____

One simple reason to be grateful for living where I live _____

_____

_____

I GIVE MYSELF PERMISSION NOT
TO RUSH THINGS INTO PLACE. THERE IS
ENOUGH TIME FOR EVERYTHING.

We do not know what is coming.
Life is beautiful anyway.

– CHRISTINA BALDWIN

Something that gives my life pleasure _____

_____

_____

An ability that I am fortunate to have _____

_____

_____

A choice I can make that not everyone gets to make _____

_____

_____

The greatest benefit of being alive right now _____

_____

_____

AS I IMAGINE THE LIFE I WANT, I FALL IN
LOVE WITH THE LIFE I ALREADY HAVE.

DATE

_____ / _____ / _____

Where there is gratitude, there is the realization that we can find happiness and peace even when things are not going our way.

– ARIANNA HUFFINGTON

A time when I felt I was in the right place at the right time _____

_____

_____

Something great about today that I may have overlooked

yesterday _____

_____

Something I can experience or imagine that inspires me _____

_____

_____

A quality of one of my closest friends that I absolutely love _____

_____

_____

IN A WORLD FULL OF CHOICES,
I CHOOSE TO SEE THE GOOD.

DATE

_____ / _____ / _____

Your vision will become clear only when you can look into your heart.
Who looks outside, dreams; who looks inside, awakes.

– CARL JUNG

Something that worked out much better than I'd hoped _____

_____

_____

Something in my life that makes it worth living _____

_____

_____

Someone or something that makes me smile like a kid again _____

_____

_____

Something that went right today _____

_____

_____

I RECOGNIZE THE MANY GOOD
QUALITIES THAT I HAVE AND I
SHARE THEM WITH OTHERS.

DATE

_____ / _____ / _____

When you focus on the good,
the good gets better.

– ABRAHAM HICKS

One way my life is better now than I ever expected it to be _____

_____

_____

A challenging experience that helped me grow into a better

version of myself _____

_____

Someone I get to spend time with today _____

_____

_____

A reason to smile right now _____

_____

_____

THE MORE GRATEFUL I AM,
THE EASIER IT IS TO FIND HAPPINESS
IN THE MOMENT.

DATE

_____ / _____ / _____

Don't be quick to judge how regretful or amazing your past was,
how good or bad your present is, or how great your future will be.
Be content with now.

– NAJWA ZEBIAN

A breakdown that led me to a breakthrough _____

_____

_____

Something or someone that makes me smile like a kid again _____

_____

_____

A second chance I've been given _____

_____

_____

Something I can experience or imagine that inspires me _____

_____

_____

APPRECIATING PEOPLE,
EXPERIENCES, AND THINGS IS A NORMAL
PART OF MY EVERYDAY LIFE.

Be thankful for what you have; you'll end up having more.
If you concentrate on what you don't have,
you will never, ever have enough.

– OPRAH WINFREY

One beautiful reason to be happy right now_____

_____

_____

An unforgettable memory I treasure _____

_____

_____

Something I currently have that I've always wanted _____

_____

_____

A new door that opened for me recently _____

_____

_____

I LEAVE BEHIND OLD HABITS AND
INVITE NEW PERSPECTIVES AND FRESH
IDEAS INTO MY WORLD.

DATE

_____ / _____ / _____

I don't have to chase extraordinary moments to find happiness—it's right in front of me if I'm paying attention and practicing gratitude.

– BRENÉ BROWN

Someone who helped me get to where I am today _____

_____

_____

A sight, sound, or feeling that reminds me why life is so amazing

_____

_____

One way my life is better now than I ever expected it to be _____

_____

_____

A reason to smile right now _____

_____

_____

NO MATTER WHAT HAPPENS,
I AM ALWAYS ALL RIGHT.

DATE

_____ / _____ / _____

Gratitude doesn't change the scenery. It merely washes clean the glass you look through so you can clearly see the colors.

– RICHELLE E. GOODRICH

Someone who's given me hope on a bad day_____

_____

_____

A skill I have that benefits me in an important way _____

_____

_____

What I love most about my community _____

_____

_____

Someone whose presence makes my life sweeter _____

_____

_____

THIS IS MY MOMENT. EVERY SINGLE STEP
AND MISSTEP HAS LED ME HERE.

DATE

_____ / _____ / _____

When you wake up every day, you have two choices.
You can either be positive or negative; an optimist or a pessimist.
I choose to be an optimist.

– HARVEY MACKAY

One reason today makes me look forward to tomorrow_____

_____

_____

One of the best parts about being me _____

_____

_____

Something I currently have that I've always wanted _____

_____

_____

A new door that opened for me recently _____

_____

_____

I CAN'T ALWAYS CONTROL WHAT HAPPENS
ON THE OUTSIDE, BUT I CAN ALWAYS CONTROL
HOW I PERCEIVE IT ON THE INSIDE.

DATE

_____ / _____ / _____

There is always something to be grateful for . . . The skies burst open, and torrential rain "ruins" your day, and out of the blue, there is torrential gratitude for the water that allows life to flourish.

– JEFF FOSTER

What I appreciate most about this moment _____

_____

_____

Something about me that's worth celebrating _____

_____

_____

An opportunity I have today that I only dreamt about having

previously _____

_____

Someone who helped me get to where I am today _____

_____

_____

I CAN FEEL IT . . .
TODAY IS THE START
OF SOMETHING GOOD.

DATE

_____ / _____ / _____

*I have noticed that people are dealing too much with the negative,
with what is wrong . . . Why not try the other way . . . to see positive
things, to just touch those things and make them bloom?*

– THICH NHAT HANH

Something I wake up to that reminds me what a gift it is to be alive

_____

_____

One way I am already living the life I want _____

_____

_____

Someone who's given me hope on a bad day _____

_____

_____

A second chance I've been given _____

_____

_____

EVERYTHING HAPPENS FOR A
REASON AND SEASON. I DON'T REGRET
ANYTHING IN MY LIFE.

DATE

_____ / _____ / _____

When you rise in the morning, give thanks for the light,
for your life, for your strength . . . If you see no reason
to give thanks, the fault lies in yourself.

– TECUMSEH

One clear reason to appreciate the person I've become _____

_____

_____

One simple reason to be grateful for living where I live _____

_____

_____

A time I felt I was in the right place at the right time _____

_____

_____

Something great about today that I may have overlooked

yesterday _____

_____

I FILL MY LIFE WITH PEOPLE,
PLACES, AND CONVERSATIONS THAT
MAKE ME FEEL GOOD.

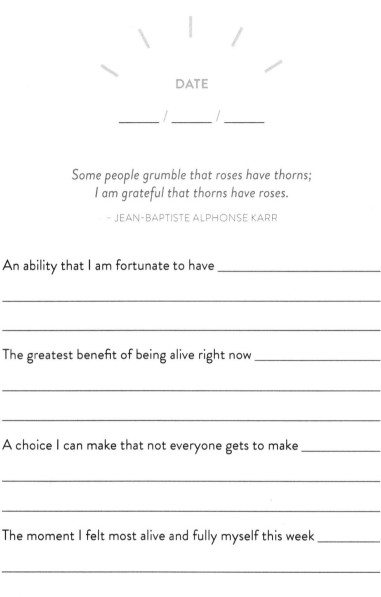

DATE

_____ / _____ / _____

Some people grumble that roses have thorns;
I am grateful that thorns have roses.

– JEAN-BAPTISTE ALPHONSE KARR

An ability that I am fortunate to have _____

_____

_____

The greatest benefit of being alive right now _____

_____

_____

A choice I can make that not everyone gets to make _____

_____

_____

The moment I felt most alive and fully myself this week _____

_____

_____

THERE ARE SO MANY WONDERFUL
REASONS TO BE GRATEFUL.

DATE

_____ / _____ / _____

You need to learn how to select your thoughts just the same way you select your clothes every day. This is a power you can cultivate.

– ELIZABETH GILBERT

One reason my life is already great _____

_____

_____

Something about myself I would never change _____

_____

_____

A reason to smile right now _____

_____

_____

Something I currently have that I've always wanted _____

_____

_____

IN THE SPACE BETWEEN WHERE I AM
AND WHERE I WANT TO BE, I THRIVE.

DATE

_____ / _____ / _____

I accept and love who I used to be. I accept and love who I am now.
I accept and love who I will become.

– FRANCES CANNON

I felt I was in the right place at the right time when _____

_____

_____

One reason today makes me look forward to tomorrow _____

_____

_____

An unforgettable memory I treasure _____

_____

_____

A quality of one of my closest friends that I absolutely love _____

_____

_____

IT IS EASY FOR ME TO BE GRATEFUL
FOR THE SMALL THINGS, LIKE THE SOUND
OF LAUGHTER, A CALL FROM A FRIEND,
OR THE WARM SUN ON MY FACE.

Be happy for this moment.
This moment is your life.

– OMAR KHAYYAM

What I love most about my community _____

_____

_____

Something that went right today _____

_____

_____

Something about myself I would never change _____

_____

_____

A new door that opened for me recently _____

_____

_____

CALM, CLARITY,
AND PEACE OF MIND
ARE A NATURAL PART
OF MY LIFE.

DATE

_____ / _____ / _____

Gratitude makes sense of our past, brings peace for today,
and creates a vision for tomorrow.

– MELODY BEATTIE

A sight, sound, or feeling that reminds me why life is so amazing

_____

_____

One way my life is better now than I ever expected it to be _____

_____

_____

A challenging experience that helped me grow into a better

version of myself _____

_____

Someone I get to spend time with today _____

_____

_____

MY HEART IS OPEN, MY MIND IS
AT PEACE, AND ALL IS WELL.

Complaining about our problems is our greatest addiction.
Break the habit. Talk about your joys.

– RITA SCHIANO

The best moment of today _____

_____

_____

A privilege I have that, until now, I've taken for granted _____

_____

_____

Something uplifting that someone said or did _____

_____

_____

A breakdown that led me to a breakthrough _____

_____

_____

I CHOOSE TO SEE MY MISTAKES
AS AN EXPERIENCE TO LEARN FROM.

DATE

_____ / _____ / _____

Sometimes the best things are right in front of you;
it just takes some time to see them.

– GLADYS KNIGHT

One simple reason to be grateful for living where I live _____

_____

_____

A time I felt I was in the right place at the right time _____

_____

_____

Something great about today that I may have overlooked

yesterday _____

_____

The greatest benefit of being alive right now _____

_____

_____

TODAY IS THE
VERY FIRST DAY OF THE REST
OF MY LIFE.

DATE

_____ / _____ / _____

The home you have is all you need to shelter your dreams. Now.
Not tomorrow or next year.

– SARAH BAN BREATHNACH

A person, place, or thing that makes my life easier and happier ____

_____

_____

A quality of one of my closest friends that I absolutely love _____

_____

_____

What I appreciate most about this moment _____

_____

_____

An opportunity I have today that I only dreamt about having

previously _____

_____

I WELCOME THE CHANCE TO
LEARN, TAKE RISKS, MAKE MISTAKES, AND
GET UP EVEN AFTER I FALL.

DATE

_____ / _____ / _____

*I'm grateful for being here, for being able to think, for being able
to see, for being able to taste, for appreciating love . . . I'm grateful to
know that it exists.*

– MAYA ANGELOU

Something about me that's worth celebrating _____

_____

_____

Someone who helped me get to where I am today _____

_____

_____

A sight, sound, or feeling that reminds me why life is so amazing

_____

_____

One way my life is better now than I ever expected it to be _____

_____

_____

MY LIFE IS ALWAYS GETTING BETTER.
I AM ALWAYS GETTING BETTER.

DATE

_____ / _____ / _____

I'm grateful for past betrayals, heartaches, and challenges . . .
I thought they were breaking me, but they were sculpting me.

– STEVE MARABOLI

Someone I get to spend time with today _____

_____

_____

A reason to smile right now _____

_____

_____

A valuable lesson I learned from a difficult situation _____

_____

_____

Something that went right today _____

_____

_____

JOY IS EVERYWHERE
I CHOOSE TO SEE IT.

DATE

_____ / _____ / _____

I have too many flaws to be perfect.
But I have too many blessings to be ungrateful.

– UNKNOWN

Something I wake up to that reminds me what a gift it is to be alive

_____

_____

One way I am already living the life I want _____

_____

_____

Someone who's given me hope on a bad day _____

_____

_____

A privilege I have that, until now, I've taken for granted _____

_____

_____

MY LIFE IS PLENTIFUL
AND MY DAYS ARE FULL OF REASONS
TO SMILE.

DATE

_____ / _____ / _____

*Gratitude is the single most important ingredient
to living a successful and fulfilled life.*

– JACK CANFIELD

Someone or something that makes me smile like a kid again _____

_____

_____

One clear reason to appreciate the person I've become _____

_____

_____

Something I can experience or imagine that inspires me _____

_____

_____

A little thing someone did that meant a lot to me _____

_____

_____

WHEN I REALLY STOP AND LOOK,
I SEE THAT THINGS USUALLY TURN OUT BETTER
THAN I COULD HAVE IMAGINED.

DATE

_____ / _____ / _____

Your mantra is thank you. Just keep saying thank you.
Don't explain. Don't complain. Just say thank you.
Say thank you to existence.

– MOOJI

Someone I don't want to miss an opportunity to say thank you to

_____

_____

A recent event that confirms that things are working out for me

_____

_____

Something that gives my life meaning _____

_____

_____

A choice I can make that not everyone gets to make _____

_____

_____

 I SEE THE BEST THAT EXISTS IN OTHERS, AND
THEY SEE AND BRING OUT THE BEST IN ME.

DATE

_____ / _____ / _____

*Do not spoil what you have by desiring what you have not;
remember that what you now have was once
among the things you only hoped for.*

– EPICURUS

The greatest benefit of being alive right now _____

_____

_____

The moment I felt most alive and fully myself this week _____

_____

_____

A need I have that is being met today _____

_____

_____

Something that gives my life pleasure _____

_____

_____

NO MATTER HOW HARD THINGS GET,
THERE IS ALWAYS SOMEONE I CAN RELY ON
TO HELP ME.

DATE

_____ / _____ / _____

Gratitude is the
memory of the heart.

– JEAN-BAPTISTE MASSIEU

One simple reason to be grateful for living where I live _____

_____

_____

A breakdown that led me to a breakthrough _____

_____

_____

One way my life is better now than I ever expected it to be _____

_____

_____

Something great about today that I may have overlooked

yesterday _____

_____

MY LIFE IS FULL OF OPTIONS.
I AM THANKFUL FOR MY FREEDOM MORE
AND MORE EACH DAY.

DATE

_____ / _____ / _____

Be willing to be blind to all your tomorrows.
A day, fully lived, will always be more than enough. Gratitude is
the key, and the lock was never made.

– JEFF FOSTER

Something I believe in that gives me hope day to day _____

_____

_____

The best moment of today _____

_____

_____

A second chance I've been given _____

_____

_____

Something uplifting that someone said or did _____

_____

_____

IN A WORLD WHERE
I CAN BE ANYTHING, I CHOOSE
TO BE GRATEFUL.

DATE

_____ / _____ / _____

One appreciates that daily life is really good when one wakes from a horrible dream . . . Why not realize it now?

– WILLIAM LYON PHELPS

An experience I cherish because it taught me something valuable

_____

_____

Something or someone that made today a good day _____

_____

_____

An ability that I am fortunate to have _____

_____

_____

Something I have that makes it easy to love my life _____

_____

_____

I AM FALLING IN LOVE
WITH THE JOURNEY OF LIFE.

DATE

_____ / _____ / _____

Gratitude and attitude are not challenges;
they are choices.

– ROBERT BRAATHE

A challenging experience that helped me grow into a better

version of myself _____

_____

Something great about today that makes me look forward to

tomorrow _____

_____

Someone who makes my life better just by being in it _____

_____

_____

One of the best parts about being me _____

_____

_____

I MOVE THROUGH THIS DAY
GENTLY AND EASILY.

DATE

_____ / _____ / _____

*Practice awareness that everything is gift,
everything is gratuitous, and if it's all given, gratuitously given,
then the only appropriate response is gratefulness.*

– DAVID STEINDL-RAST

Something I currently have that I've always wanted _____

_____

_____

A new door that opened for me recently _____

_____

_____

So far, what I love most about today _____

_____

_____

One simple pleasure I value _____

_____

_____

THERE IS SO MUCH
BEAUTY IN EVERY MINUTE
OF MY LIFE.

DATE

_____ / _____ / _____

Change the way you look at things,
and the things you look at change.

– WAYNE DYER

One beautiful reason to be happy right now _____

_____

_____

A skill I have that benefits me in an important way _____

_____

_____

What I love most about my community _____

_____

_____

A quality of one of my closest friends that I absolutely love _____

_____

_____

EVERY DAY, I CREATE NEW HABITS
THAT GET ME CLOSER TO WHERE AND
WHO I WANT TO BE.

DATE

_____ / _____ / _____

When you arise in the morning, think of what a privilege it is
to be alive, to breathe, to think, to enjoy, to love.

– MARCUS AURELIUS

A routine that gives my life meaning _____

_____

_____

A challenging experience that helped me grow into a better

version of myself _____

_____

An unforgettable memory I treasure _____

_____

_____

Something about myself I would never change _____

_____

_____

MY LIFE IS FILLED WITH STRONG,
SUPPORTIVE, LOVING RELATIONSHIPS
WITH FAMILY AND FRIENDS.

DATE

_____ / _____ / _____

Want what you have, and then
you can have what you want.

– FREDERICK DODSON

Something that worked out much better than I'd hoped _____

_____

_____

A reason to smile right now _____

_____

_____

Someone whose presence makes my life sweeter _____

_____

_____

Something in my life that makes it worth living _____

_____

_____

LIFE SUPPORTS
ME IN ALL THE WAYS
I NEED.

DATE

_____ / _____ / _____

When you're looking for joy,
you'll always find it hiding in gratitude.

– UNKNOWN

Something I get to do today that I've always wanted to do _____

_____

_____

One reason I cherish this time of year _____

_____

_____

A freedom I have that I once took for granted _____

_____

_____

The best part of today _____

_____

_____

I AM OVERFLOWING WITH GRATITUDE,
AND MY HEART IS FULL.

DATE

_____ / _____ / _____

*Nothing is more powerful than allowing yourself to be truly affected
by things. Whether it's a song, a stranger, a mountain, a rain drop . . .
All of this is for you. Take it and have gratitude. Give it and feel love.*

– AMELIA OLSON

A quality of one of my closest friends that I absolutely love _____

_____

_____

What I appreciate most about this moment _____

_____

_____

An opportunity I have today that I only dreamt about having

previously _____

_____

Something about me that's worth celebrating _____

_____

_____

I GIVE MYSELF PERMISSION TO DO
WHAT MAKES ME HAPPY.

*If it sounds good and it feels good,
then it is good!*

– DUKE ELLINGTON

One way I am already living the life I want _____

_____

_____

An unforgettable memory I treasure _____

_____

_____

One of the best parts about being me _____

_____

_____

Something I currently have that I've always wanted _____

_____

_____

I AM FLEXIBLE, FLUID,
AND LIVING IN HARMONY WITH LIFE.

DATE

_____ / _____ / _____

Those with a grateful mindset tend to see the message in the mess. And even though life may knock them down, the grateful find reasons, if even small ones, to get up.

– STEVE MARABOLI

Someone who helped me get to where I am today _____

_____

_____

A sight, sound, or feeling that reminds me why life is so amazing

_____

_____

One way my life is better now than I ever expected it to be _____

_____

_____

A challenging experience that helped me grow into a better

version of myself _____

_____

AS I INVITE APPRECIATION TO STAY, FEAR,
DOUBT, AND WORRY NATURALLY FALL AWAY.

DATE

_____ / _____ / _____

When we look at what's satisfied us in the past week or month or decade, it's been the connections, the love and the openness of our lives to the places we've traveled and the people we've met. This really is the basis for gratitude.

– JACK KORNFIELD

Someone I get to spend time with today _____

_____

_____

A reason to smile right now _____

_____

_____

A valuable lesson I learned from a difficult situation _____

_____

_____

Something that went right today _____

_____

_____

I AM GRATEFUL FOR
EVERY CHALLENGING MOMENT.
EVERY MOMENT IS MY TEACHER.

DATE

_____ / _____ / _____

Happy, wholly healthy people must dance on the edge of the fine line between getting clear on what they desire and being grateful for what they already have.

– LISSA RANKIN

A time I felt I was in the right place at the right time _____

_____

_____

Something great about today that I may have overlooked

yesterday _____

_____

A little thing someone did that meant a lot to me _____

_____

_____

Someone or something that made today a good day _____

_____

_____

I AM AT EASE WITH BOTH MY
STRENGTH AND MY LIMITS, MY SUCCESSES
AND MY CHALLENGES.

DATE

_____ / _____ / _____

Gratitude leads to joy. When you count your blessings on a regular basis, they will multiply many, many times over.

– CHRISTIANE NORTHRUP

Someone I don't want to miss an opportunity to say thank you to

_____

_____

A recent event that confirms that things are working out for me

_____

_____

Something that gives my life meaning _____

_____

_____

A choice I can make that not everyone gets to make _____

_____

_____

EVERY DAY MAY NOT BE PERFECT, BUT THERE
IS SOMETHING PERFECT IN EVERY DAY.

DATE

_____ / _____ / _____

For the yesterdays and todays, and the tomorrows
I can hardly wait for—thank you.

– CECELIA AHERN

The greatest benefit of being alive right now _____
_____
_____

The moment I felt most alive and fully myself this week _____
_____
_____

A need I have that is being met today _____
_____
_____

An ability that I am fortunate to have _____
_____
_____

I CELEBRATE ALL THAT I AM AND ALL
THAT I BRING TO THE WORLD.

DATE

_____ / _____ / _____

If you can't change the situation, change how you feel about it.

– UNKNOWN

Something I wake up to that reminds me what a gift it is to be alive

_____

_____

One way I am already living the life I want _____

_____

_____

Someone who's given me hope on a bad day _____

_____

_____

A choice I can make that not everyone gets to make _____

_____

_____

I GIVE THANKS
TO AND DANCE WITH THE FLOW
OF MY LIFE.

DATE

_____ / _____ / _____

Love those who appreciate you, and appreciate those who love you.

– CONNOR CHALFANT

The best moment of today _____

_____

_____

A privilege I have that, until now, I've taken for granted _____

_____

_____

A breakdown that led me to a breakthrough _____

_____

_____

A second chance I've been given _____

_____

_____

MY TRUST IN MYSELF AND IN LIFE IS
CONSTANTLY INCREASING. EVERYTHING
IS AS IT SHOULD BE.

DATE

_____ / _____ / _____

*Truly appreciate those around you,
and you'll soon find many others around you.*

– RALPH MARSTON

Something uplifting that someone said or did _____

_____

_____

An experience I cherish because it taught me something valuable

_____

_____

One clear reason to appreciate the person I've become _____

_____

_____

Something that makes me smile like a kid again _____

_____

_____

I SEE SO MUCH TO BE THANKFUL
FOR AND I KNOW, WITHOUT A DOUBT,
THAT LIFE IS WORTH LIVING.

DATE

_____ / _____ / _____

For one minute, walk outside, stand there in silence.
Look up at the sky and contemplate how amazing life is.

– UNKNOWN

Something I can experience or imagine that inspires me _____

_____

_____

One simple reason to be grateful for living where I live _____

_____

_____

Something that gives my life pleasure _____

_____

_____

So far, what I love most about today _____

_____

_____

TODAY IS RIPE WITH
NEW BEGINNINGS AND
FRESH STARTS.

DATE

_____ / _____ / _____

I am thankful for my struggle because without it,
I wouldn't have stumbled across my strength.

– UNKNOWN

One reason my life is already great _____

_____

_____

A skill I have that benefits me in an important way _____

_____

_____

Someone whose presence makes my life sweeter _____

_____

_____

A beautiful reason to be happy right now _____

_____

_____

WHEN MY APPRECIATION
IS PLENTIFUL, MY JOY
IS INEVITABLE.

DATE

_____ / _____ / _____

Gratitude unlocks the fullness of life. It turns what we have into enough, and more . . . Gratitude makes sense of our past, brings peace for today, and creates a vision for tomorrow.

– MELODY BEATTIE

Something I get to do today that I've always wanted to do _____

_____

_____

One simple pleasure I value _____

_____

_____

The best part of today _____

_____

_____

A recent event that confirms that things are working out for me

_____

_____

I NO LONGER WORRY ABOUT WHAT
COULD GO WRONG. I FOCUS, INSTEAD,
ON ALL THAT IS RIGHT.

*Give every day the chance to become
the most beautiful day of your life.*

– MARK TWAIN

One reason I cherish this time of year _____

_____

_____

A freedom I have that I once took for granted _____

_____

_____

What I love most about my community _____

_____

_____

Someone who helped me get to where I am today _____

_____

_____

I AM LETTING CLARITY, APPRECIATION,
AND CONFIDENCE LEAD THE WAY.

DATE

_____ / _____ / _____

*Gratitude paints little smiley faces
on everything it touches.*

– RICHELLE E. GOODRICH

A new door that opened for me recently _____

_____

_____

Someone who makes my life better just by being in it _____

_____

_____

A person or thing that makes my life easier and happier _____

_____

_____

Something that worked out much better than I'd hoped _____

_____

_____

THERE IS SO MUCH ABOUT
LIFE THAT I LOVE.

DATE

_____ / _____ / _____

I am so glad you are here.
It helps me realize how beautiful my world is.

– RAINER MARIA RILKE

Something about myself I would never change _____

_____

_____

Something in my life that makes it worth living _____

_____

_____

One reason today makes me look forward to tomorrow _____

_____

_____

A sight, sound, or feeling that reminds me why life is so amazing

_____

_____

 I SEE MY LIFE, AND THE WORLD IN WHICH
I LIVE, WITH GRATEFUL EYES.

DATE

_____ / _____ / _____

*Enjoy the little things in life, for one day you
may look back and realize they were the big things.*

– UNKNOWN

Something I can experience or imagine that inspires me _____

_____

_____

One simple reason to be grateful for living where I live _____

_____

_____

A routine that gives my life pleasure _____

_____

_____

What I love most about today _____

_____

_____

I CAN BE HAPPY WHENEVER I WANT
NO MATTER WHAT MY CIRCUMSTANCES.

DATE

_____ / _____ / _____

This is a wonderful day.
I've never seen this one before.

– MAYA ANGELOU

Something in my life that makes it worth living _____

_____

_____

A quality of one of my closest friends that I absolutely love _____

_____

_____

What I appreciate most about this moment _____

_____

_____

An opportunity I have today that I only dreamt about having

previously _____

_____

I BELIEVE IN MY ABILITY TO RIDE THE WAVES
OF SHIFT AND CHANGE WITH EASE.

DATE

_____ / _____ / _____

The thing that's worth doing is trying to improve our understanding of the world and gain a better appreciation of the universe . . . Because actually, life's pretty good. It really is.

– ELON MUSK

Someone who helped me get to where I am today _____

_____

_____

A sight, sound, or feeling that reminds me why life is so amazing

_____

_____

One way my life is better now than I ever expected it to be _____

_____

_____

A challenging experience that helped me grow into a better

version of myself _____

_____

TODAY WILL BE
ANOTHER GREAT DAY.

DATE

_____ / _____ / _____

Some days there won't be a song in your heart. Sing anyway.

– EMORY AUSTIN

Someone I get to spend time with today _____

_____

_____

A reason to smile right now _____

_____

_____

A valuable lesson I learned from a difficult situation _____

_____

_____

Something that went right today _____

_____

_____

I AM IN TUNE WITH
MYSELF AND IN SYNC WITH MY
SURROUNDINGS.

DATE

_____ / _____ / _____

Gratitude can turn common days into thanksgivings.

– WILLIAM ARTHUR WARD

Something I wake up to that reminds me what a gift it is to be alive

_____

_____

One way I am already living the life I want _____

_____

_____

Someone who's given me hope on a bad day _____

_____

_____

Something I believe in that gives me hope day to day _____

_____

_____

I EXPECT ALL SETBACKS TO TURN
INTO COMEBACKS, AND ALL BREAKDOWNS
TO TURN INTO BREAKTHROUGHS.

DATE

_____ / _____ / _____

Mind is a flexible mirror,
adjust it, to see a better world.

– AMIT RAY

A privilege I have that, until now, I've taken for granted _____

_____

_____

Something uplifting that someone said _____

_____

_____

One reason to appreciate the person I've become _____

_____

_____

Something that made today a good day _____

_____

_____

IT'S TRUE . . . ONCE I ONLY DREAMED
OF BEING WHERE I AM NOW.

DATE

_____ / _____ / _____

More smiling, less worrying. More compassion, less judgment.
More blessed, less stressed. More love, less hate.

– ROY T. BENNETT

A recent event that confirms that things are working out for me

_____

_____

Something that gives my life meaning _____

_____

_____

An ability that I am fortunate to have _____

_____

_____

The greatest benefit of being alive right now _____

_____

_____

LOVE, JOY, AND SINCERE GRATITUDE
ARE A NATURAL PART OF WHO I AM.

DATE

_____ / _____ / _____

The best way to keep relationships happy, healthy,
and supportive can be summed up in one word: appreciation.

– MARCI SHIMOFF

A breakdown that led me to a breakthrough _____

_____

_____

Someone whose presence makes my life sweeter _____

_____

_____

An experience that taught me something valuable _____

_____

_____

A time I felt I was in the right place at the right time _____

_____

_____

APPRECIATION SPREADS THROUGH
MY THOUGHTS AND ACTIONS AND
FLOWS INTO MY WORLD.

DATE

_____ / _____ / _____

If you're reading this . . . congratulations, you're alive. If that's not something to smile about, then I don't know what is.

– CHAD SUGG

A second chance I've been given _____

_____

_____

Someone I get to spend time with today _____

_____

_____

One reason to be grateful for living where I live _____

_____

_____

A little thing someone did that meant a lot to me _____

_____

_____

I HAVE THE POWER
TO CREATE POSITIVE,
LASTING CHANGE.

DATE

_____ / _____ / _____

*Keep your head high, keep your chin up,
and most importantly, keep smiling, because life's a
beautiful thing and there's so much to smile about.*

– MARILYN MONROE

Someone I don't want to miss an opportunity to say thank you to

_____

_____

A choice I am grateful that I get to make _____

_____

_____

The moment I felt most alive and fully myself this week _____

_____

_____

A need I have that is being met today _____

_____

_____

I KNOW MYSELF,
I TRUST MYSELF, AND
I CAN BE MYSELF.

DATE

_____ / _____ / _____

*Live each day as if your
life had just begun.*

– JOHANN WOLFGANG VON GOETHE

One beautiful reason to be happy right now _____

_____

_____

A skill I have that benefits me in an important way _____

_____

_____

One reason I cherish this time of year _____

_____

_____

What I love most about my community _____

_____

_____

I AM A MUCH KINDER,
HAPPIER VERSION OF ME. AND
I'VE ONLY JUST BEGUN.

DATE

_____ / _____ / _____

*Live with intention. Walk to the edge. Listen hard.
Practice wellness. Play with abandon. Laugh. Choose with
no regret. Appreciate your friends. Continue to learn.
Do what you love. Live as if this is all there is.*

– MARY ANNE RADMACHER

Something I wake up to that reminds me what a gift it is to be alive

_____

_____

Something about myself I would never change _____

_____

_____

One reason my life is already great _____

_____

_____

Someone whose presence makes my life sweeter _____

_____

_____

MY STRESS IS DECREASING;
MY PEACE OF MIND IS INCREASING.

DATE

_____ / _____ / _____

You cannot always control what goes on outside.
But you can always control what goes on inside.

– WAYNE DYER

Something I get to do today that I've always wanted to do _____

_____

_____

A simple pleasure I value _____

_____

_____

The best part of today _____

_____

_____

A little thing someone did that meant a lot to me _____

_____

_____

I LIKE WHO I'VE BECOME AND AM EXCITED
ABOUT THE PERSON I AM BECOMING.

DATE

_____ / _____ / _____

I look out the window and I see the lights and the skyline
and the people on the street rushing around looking for action,
love . . . and my heart does a little dance.

– NORA EPHRON

One reason my life is already great _____

_____

_____

Something great about today that I may have overlooked

yesterday _____

_____

One clear reason to appreciate the person I've become _____

_____

_____

A privilege I have that, until now, I've taken for granted _____

_____

_____

MY LIFE IS MOVING FORWARD
IN THE MOST WONDERFUL WAY.

DATE

_____ / _____ / _____

The greatest discovery of all time
is that a person can change his future by
merely changing his attitude.

– OPRAH WINFREY

A little thing someone did that meant a lot to me _____

_____

_____

A new opportunity I've been given _____

_____

_____

Something that gives my life meaning _____

_____

_____

What I appreciate most about this moment _____

_____

_____

I APPROACH TODAY
WITH AN OPEN HEART.

DATE

_____ / _____ / _____

When we focus on our gratitude, the tide of
disappointment goes out and the tide of love rushes in.

– KRISTIN ARMSTRONG

A challenging experience that helped me grow into a better

version of myself _____

_____

What went right today _____

_____

_____

A person, place, or thing that makes my life easier and happier

_____

_____

Something I currently have that I've always wanted _____

_____

_____

I AM LOVING THE LIFE I LIVE.

DATE

_____ / _____ / _____

Appreciate every little beautiful moment in every day of your life.
Give it a try and you'll see the world from another perspective.

– THEA KRISTINE MAY

An ability that I am fortunate to have _____

_____

_____

Someone whose presence makes my life sweeter _____

_____

_____

A need I have that is being met today _____

_____

_____

The greatest benefit of being alive right now _____

_____

_____

THIS MOMENT IS WHERE LIFE HAPPENS.
THIS MOMENT IS MORE THAN ENOUGH.

Acknowledgments

Not unlike the pages of this journal, its author is bursting with gratitude, too.

First and foremost, for the many cumulative moments of laughter, love, and growth and for being the sisters of my soul, keepers of my dreams, and best friends of my heart, a huge thank you to Tieg Alexander, Kristen Chazaud, and Kristen Petrillo.

To Tieg Alexander, thank you for being my wise, beloved friend and sounding board. I am beyond grateful for the events that brought us together and remain happily astonished at how there is no end to the unconditional love, balance, reciprocity, and "a-has" that I learn from and share with you.

For the intuitive connection that led to a wonderfully nourishing friendship, the conversation that led to the Happiness Doctor, and for all that's beautifully transpired since and all that's yet to come, I cherish you so much, Kristen Chazaud.

To Kristen Petrillo, I can't thank you enough, homie, for being wild, wonderful, kindhearted you and for loving wild, wonderful, and kindhearted me. I am so thankful to have you in my life.

Thank you to Margaret Schneider for teaching me to become a better writer and woman through guidance, modeling, and gentle support. And to the many mentors who've played an important role in my personal and professional journey, including Marci Lobel and Joanne Zinger, I am so incredibly grateful.

Deep appreciation to Laura Khait, for your many years of listening, your kindness, compassion, and ever-present open heart. And to Inna Breslin, who has been a source of gratitude since day one.

Thank you to all of the teachers and experiences—from Shambhala meditation at the Center for Living Peace and energy medicine and yoga studies and practices in Southern California to inner explorations in Costa Rica, cross-country road trips, and international teaching adventures—that sparked and maintained my passion and curiosity for that juicy, authentic, "can't buy it in a store" kind of joy.

For the seeds of transformation planted with you, Suyana Cole, conscious conversations had with you, Sorinne Ardeleanu, and conscious explorations shared with you, Drew Gerald—I am so thankful.

A special thank you to Karl Mertens, Juliel Lynn, Warren Greaves, Illya Engle, Luca Crespi, and all of the wonderful people that give me so much gratitude for the place I call home—my world is better because you are in it.

Bountiful thanks to Elizabeth Castoria for the invitation to turn the musings of my mind and heart into a gratitude journal. And to Sean Newcott, for each moment of encouragement and presence, and your editing prowess, too. And to Lisa Forde, for the beautiful design that made my words come to life.

A special shout-out also to my remarkable and courageous clients—for being an ongoing source of learning, humility, and inspiration, and for allowing me to see me in you and you in me.

And to my inspiring colleagues and friends, especially Andy Viar, Caroline Whisman-Blair, Laura Parker, and the Internal Family Systems community, who continuously help me learn how to soften my heart and befriend my mind more and more each day. It is from those spaces that these words were written.

Deepest of all, my wholehearted thanks to Izabella, Anatoly, and Oleg Bershadsky for your lifetime of love and support. Your encouragement of my intellectual passions and support of my often nontraditional life choices and aspirations fueled my deter-mination to create and live a life I truly love. You are always close to my heart, as I live, as I love, and as I write.

About the Author

Sophia Godkin, PhD, is a health psychologist, happyologist, and happiness, relationship, and transformational coach. Through integrated coaching, interactive education, and customized consulting, Sophia helps people adopt the perspectives, behaviors, and habits that lead to fulfilling careers, rewarding relationships, and a life full of growth, authenticity, and endless possibility. As an educator at numerous wellness companies and universities, Sophia has taught the principles and practices of happiness, health, and conscious living all around the world. Whether it be individual coaching, writing, or group education, Sophia's work is known for its depth, lightheartedness, and transformative potential.

When Sophia's not busy helping people create a healthier, happier life, she loves walking and biking outdoors; camping and hiking; salsa and bachata dancing; practicing yoga; paddling in Idaho's beautiful ponds and lakes; nourishing her emotional and intellectual self through reading, music, and reflective practices; and enjoying each moment of being alive in the company of the amazing people she calls friends. Visit her online at TheHappinessDoctor.com.

CPSIA information can be obtained
at www.ICGtesting.com
Printed in the USA
JSHW042142210221
11954JS00005B/22